A Wild Rain

poems by

Margaret Rooney

Finishing Line Press
Georgetown, Kentucky

A Wild Rain

I dedicate this book to my sister Briahn Kelly-Brennan. She opened the possibility of poetry, for me, persuaded me to walk into its wide embrace and fall in love with its grasp of voice and story. I also want to express my gratitude and love to Larry Mattics, Peter Mattaroo, Brianne Wise, Peter Rooney and Carlos di Lima for their unstinting support and encouragement. And to thank my three poetry groups of wise, accomplished women who inspire and encourage me everyday.

ACKNOWLEDGMENTS

Grateful acknowledgment is given to the following publications in which the
following poems first appeared:

Ekphrasis Vol.8 No. 3 Spring/Summer 2019—Tangled
Crow 2019—Listen, My Grandmother's Garden
And Yet 2020—On Wings of Osier and Wax
Beyond Distance 2021—Under the Soft Eye of Morning, Amidst the Ruins, Alone and
Awake, A Measure of Sorrow
RWW 2021 Poetry Prize—Prerogatives of Flight

I want to dedicate this book to my sister Briahn Kelly-Brennan. We are sisters and
poets together. She held open the possibility of poetry for me, persuaded me to walk
into its wide embrace and fall in love with its tall, wide grasp of voice and story. I
also want to express my gratitude and love for my three enduring poetry groups, who
inspire and encourage me in every way—a community of generous, deeply talented
women who have honed my skills, fostered my taste and promoted my joy.

Publisher: Leah Huete de Maines
Editor: Christen Kincaid
Cover Art: B. Kelly Brennan
Author Photo: Brianne Wise
Cover Design: Elizabeth Maines McCleavy

Order online: www.finishinglinepress.com
also available on amazon.com

Author inquiries and mail orders:
Finishing Line Press
PO Box 1626
Georgetown, Kentucky 40324
USA

Contents

From the First Burnt Offering

to the final annihilation
spills the green soul
a waterfall of light
folded into the whole
predicament of being alive

between cock-crow morning
and star-crowned night
between forest's dancing roof
and heaven's bluest arch
lies the far acre where logic fails
and imagination flies

where gods ancient and new are born
and the dead awake from their narrow vault
to join the gambol of transformation

music inverts sorrow
in all fresh starts

a favorite place of time
is that edge of beginning:

the shallows of a fish-full estuary
soft and silty carrying the wet smile of a dolphin
the first upward flange of a mountain
its unexpected thrust
after all the coasting flatness

oh and the precipice of love
full tingly and blurry
where touch is fire and
lovers live solely
on air and anticipation

where even the wind wringing
cold holds a holiness
perhaps there is an unentered door
where every heart is wide open and singing

The Howl of Poetry

I'm the mad alive woman
flung into windmills of time
chancing the quicksilver moment
and the one carefully
writing it down
in dusky silence
I'm Hafiz dancing
in his doorway inviting the world
into a joyful, loving universe
and I court death like a paramour
testing its promise of oblivion:
past the pain a porcelain stillness
sky-climbing poet atop the tower
I tease the airborne instant
on hard-boned wings
the air is electric
I can feel the pulse
of polarities
taste the livewire
incandescence
as words ignite

Nights These Days

expatriated from the warm center of things
under a sky of querulous birds
I walk along a trail of bare winter trees

darkness slowly fills the space
between branches
the pale eye of the moon rises

I think of a time when the window
of night was open to me
I could look up into an unbreakable expanse
my sister in the grass beside me

naming our childhood constellations:
Princess's Footstool, Seven Magic Stones,
Queen's Flashing Ruby

"no, no" Mama says "that's Ursa Major,
Pleiades, Betelgeuse and you forgot
the Big Shopping Cart"—she smiles—

I remember how quiet the earth was when
we were young, even quieter before we came
how clean the sky and bright the sun

we could hear the local geese loud and near
as they flew white bellied over the house
blue sky in their beaks
the meadow lark sang us awake

three lifting notes from the fencepost
we heard the mewling of new kittens
in the hay felt them all feathers and pins
their heartbeats rapid in our palms

we knew the whole world was ours
we could name it

Plastic Explosive Smells of Marzipan
(For Ukraine)

air turns bitter orange
smoke erupts from hollow windows
spools through absent ceilings

it loops and sheds upwards
sky looks badly bruised
as ash periscopes up and up

souls shapeless as water
ascend past ordinary light
we cannot tell where—

the dead are strange
and distant now
lost to touch and sound

steel-winged, dark-voweled birds
spread the terrible language of bombs
in this wordless mile

we are afraid our own small noise
might, in an instant, shatter all we know
and lives become confetti
we are an urgent desire
that dies into cracks and shadows

the bomb outruns sound
we think if we hear
its whistle we are safe

reality shifts with every wave of light
spits out caustic gases
there is only the last shock
of memory fluttering away

an old woman cries out
why are they killing the children?
the burning of everything surrounds her
books, beds and buildings

there is a plush bunny on the lawn
—there is no lawn

Edge

say you knew the sharp tip of despair
the copper taste of it
or what a person was capable of on the verge

say you heard the soft collapse of hope
leaving you breathless
under a white-boned moon

a dark angelfish
lodged in your lung
near your naked rib

all the small calamities
are nothing to this
as you pace

the circumference of fear
never quite eluding
the sting of it

knowing its echo will shrill
in your bones until you shatter
and blow its seeds everywhere

this scald of sorrow
opens a fissure in what you know
darkness creeps in like betrayal

you find yourself alone in this careful
soundless place watching the world
slip away under the grey wing of a gull

Listen

a sound
soft as breath
careful the way
it pulls the silence
around it

weaves
through the trees
like bird or sunlight
a kind of round
lowing cadence

wordless as water
with a gentle tremolo
trailing
I think it comes
from the orchard

or maybe the meadow
beyond brambled
berries
something warm
and feathered

nested in branches
hollow boned
and wakeful in the night

Stillness

laundry hangs limp
on the line this windless noon
sun burns unwavering
in a sky cloudless as Mars

indolent in the slender
shade of an olive tree
cattle done with grazing
flick flies with their tufted tails

calves curl close like furled ferns
doze softly in milk-addled daze
black-and-white dog asleep on the porch
chases cows under closed eyelids

two horses in the corral nuzzle hay
lift their heads at the slow creak
and tok-tok of the windmill
as water splashes

staccato stops and starts into
a circular steel tank
music of rising wind plays
on curved metal wings

they catch and turn
as linens on the line come alive
to shape the cotton breeze
that carries just a hint of rain

Another Bright Orchard Bulldozed

I try not to notice the bitter
itinerary of shadows
the sharp mineral smell
of uprooted earth

all the beauties stripped
from bare-buckled trees
leaves and petals curl
in pitted ground

boughs hold nothing but clouds
roots knuckle the sky
when the night is gone
pale shapes appear like skulls

in the hollows
between branch and root
white feathers of fog dislimn
what remains of the trees

a reticulation of roots pulled
out of darkness—delicacy
and density naked in air
dark soil caught in its fretwork

sound revolves in blue space
crow black as emptiness
loud as grief
looks for its lost roost

Among the Sunflowers

it is quiet among the sunflowers
is it raining? these late summer showers
flutter like white-winged moths light on green leaves
or sound loud like bees in tall stems' towers

this flowering of spring's dalliance grieves
fruited and sprung, flush and flowing with sheaves
and loaves swelling to summer's final blaze
after all is plucked, tucked and toasted leaves

us longing for that long warm summer haze
when bird-busy, cloud-full skies held our gaze
and we were firmly caught in season's thrall
and rains came lightly if they came at all

Afterlight

I sit folding and unfolding
particular sorrow bitter
as gentian purpling the air

birds dark against the sky
fly toward pale unsettled seas
adagio of half-tones
a hollow grey symphony

solitary egret etched in light
gazes with imperial grace
as two gulls shrill
over the gusty headland

facing the broad ocean
lightheaded and empty
I whisper to the wind
a rosary of regret

sorrow like water loses
its edge folds into itself
churns restless revisions
of loss and gain

rolls in and out
in tumbled
soul-shifting turns
until like the sea

its long accruals
and dispersions
alter magnitudes

In My Grandmother's Garden

old oak of prisms and pearls
rose-bedizened tea cups
and dried flower sachets
as high as the eye can reach

blue bottles green bottles
painted medicine tins
send fine tenor tones
into shifting air

palpitations of music
in ancient roots that curl
soar and dive deep in
the earth to dream of pagodas

my grandmother scaled
the oak when she was seven
even then the branches
were wide as a harvest table

and nine times as thick
she said it was like climbing
a grand staircase
on your knees

she was the one
who killed a rattler
by the front walk
when she was ninety

shot its head clean off
with the rifle she bought
from Sears Roebuck
with her egg money

A Wild Rain

in the drench of night
swept with dark
and weeping rain

a wild turkey tucked high
in the Bishop Pines calls out
to something in the wet air

here I am here I am
come here to where I am
it repeats like wind, moves lightless

as shadows, a noise weighted
with the notion of want
propagated in the sway of branches

I pray aside and slantwise too
for sunlight and redemption
circle my small transformations

and sorrows
cry in the night after
my own broken image

in the light-swindled torrent
where sound turns upon itself
and I am the only ear

hell and its superintendent
keep me from swimming
to the top of the storm where I know
an ocean of sunlit sky lies waiting

where I am the blue of the sea
color of sky's stillness
grass bent in tangled air
whistle of the walking wind

caught up in the breadth
and largeness of things I don't understand
listening through an insistent rain to the plaintive call
of a wild turkey hieratic and sacred in the pines

That Far Thing So Near

day falls around me
a colorful quilt warm
with ladders of light in trees
plaids of shadow under flowers

air is yellow with pine pollen
I am gazing through something like gauze
a thin membrane softens shapes
like an old photo or memory

I'm swimming in a sleeve of time
through an ocean of sensation
my mind slippery as a fish

is it odd then that you
should occur to me now
not intrude upon my reverie
but be my reverie

your stance loose and easy
like a young goddess
in the long-ago ripe wheat
all the golden acres unfolding

the jacket you wore
still in the closet
holds the shape of your arms

how can you not be here, too.

I know how the fields go on
they are of earth and earth endures

we, though, are like the butterflies of summer
and I have outlasted your time.

There is a Community on the Hill

a quiet place
of planted oaks and alders
lilac hedges and clipped green grass

a thousand acres of silence
surrounded by a low limestone wall
marking this circumstance of stillness

density of lives lived, undone, released
stone now holds their names
and our intention to remember

the sundial is superfluous
time is fluid here
full of shadows and leaves

soft attic light drapes every grave
here are her worn hands
his shot knees
the stillborn baby

stowaway attuned
to the rhythms
of slim chance

polished granite block
catches day's escaping light
mossy-cheeked cement angel

bends with hovered wings
as if to enfold the dead
or shelter them
under the long gaze of eternity

Alone and Awake

in an amorphous predawn
grey as dried river rock
colors hidden, near forgotten

neighbors' houses dark as slate
nearly indistinguishable
from the penumbral surround

only the slight silver
sheen of their windows
foreshadows sunrise

my eyes find a slice of moon
thinly etched in the sky above
the westernmost tree in the garden

its light softer than a firefly's
half drawn, scantily sketched
in this half-lit almost aquatic air

I float alone amongst the slumbering
dreamers imagining revisions and regrets
caught like minnows in neural nets

where odd perceptions are captured
and sideways memories migrate
where sensory images archetypal and prophetic

form frail bulwarks against fear
of the singular certainty that defines us
birth is not a given, but once born, death is

an inexorable preoccupation in this liminal space
night's hold slipping, sun's strength gathering
finality's edge sharpens
alone in the dark on the threshold of dawn

Under the Soft Eye of Morning

spoons of light
turn in the long grass
I can see everything

all at once
atom upon atom
legible as dew on a leaf

reflecting pale sky
remnant moon
and day-dimmed stars

a perishable beauty
carved out of darkness
empty space

and something like longing
on this blue speck
full of impossible stratagems

like nightjars
cocooning caterpillars
and kiting spiders

inserting themselves into time
where even imprecision
is purposeful

this mutable process
pulls me
into language

as if I could
hold this moment
that tips towards eternity

steady in my gaze
and stay the wind
that stirs the shadows

The Prerogatives of Flight

wingless on the edge of dawn
wanting to step lightly
into the purlieus of flight

lift off hollow boned and
near weightless over a tinfoil sea
untethered from solid earth

willing to give ten of my nine lives
to soar aloft rippled breezes
through open doors of air

screel along serrated cliffs
over a wrangle of waves
and tall-finned rocks

see my winged shadow
echo over the shine of estuaries
and wink of tidal marshes

chase swirl of upflow currents
pierce the wild breadth of sky
plunge headlong

into breakneck waves
against a pulling tide to emerge
with a sackful of startled fish

slip over whispering forests
and green-pitched glades
dip into folded valleys

creased with shadow
alight for an instant
on a long-leafed branch

in a balance of light and dark
sharp sound and blue silence
strung between earth and sky

Icarus On Wings of Osier and Wax

circling
a finely calibrated thought
bright budded in morning light

in one stroke
I span the world
without predicates

buoyant in shivery air
parsing density and uplift
as easy as breath

master of winds
and moon
pulled tides

on self-made
wings
of osier and wax

barefoot in revolving skies
unspun from words
or human limits

far far above
the calamitous town
with its ports and bays

curves and edges
and roundness of things
that gleam at night

long-necked boats
people consumed
by small pursuits

oblivious to rumor
of wings moving through
sky's immensities

toward that hot
unyielding orb
at caterwauling noon

in a bell of light
birds plummet
from the sky

a boat of broken things
sails through
bone-white waves

hearing the hungering
shouts of children
of gulls

sun singed
I drop
into a swallowing sea
gold lit

Wildfire

in this winding down day
green leaves blaze and shrivel
ripe seeds singe and blow

through burn-bitten air
ash upon ash of soft things and hard
furred, fleshed, footed and hooved

curls a grey cowl
round the graveyard sun
in an orange and livid sky

bark crackles in a humpbacked wind
metals melt, roofs stream flames
doorframes darken and collapse

in charred and sullied fields
the yellow teeth of corn turn black
trees smolder in unaccustomed light

stark ruined spires burn
syllables of a new language
in this fractured landscape

what does it tell us if time's intact
and the world's worn away
shorn of branch and bud

who shall be morning's stronghold
against the eroding sea
the withering wind

and guard the ramparts of the sky
when there are no gods left to us
under the world's round and wounded eye

A Measure of Sorrow

day stings like a scorpion
pushes past eyeburst light
pointed as nails
sprung as stars

she holds tatters of night
in folds of her garment
darkness doubles
at midnight

dreams canyon airless
through the mind
black holes fill
and empty like doors

memory floats
in eddies and pools
turns like a leaf folding
in and out of dark and bright

faces half remembered
half felt like the silk
of petals on fingertips

she wants to hold on to things
but they slip away on a current
she cannot see

there is an innumerable loss
she wants to mark
with smooth round stones

piled one upon another
making a mountain of them
to hail this deafening silence

every day is filled
with the sound
of lost footsteps

When Love Alters

do I return to you in memory
wafted on wind
stirred by drifts of light
or something skirting knowledge

that sultry summer
we walked under the cool
shifting shadows
of Linden trees

aware of deeply veined bark
dark twined branches
white flower clusters
like feathers or knots of snow

aware of each other's breath
my hand warm in yours
quietly on fire

in cadences of sunlight
spun on wheels of desire
we dare everything

trust circling planets
folding seas
the rolling flight of a gull

you occur to me now
sometimes

when leaves turn
silver in moonlight
and edges disappear

Tangled

we inhabit the voluptuous
stillness of an afternoon wood
air smooth as watered silk
leaves intricate as Belgian lace

adorned with seed-pearl sprays
glimmers of blue sky play
through the vaulting green
I taste the weight of sunlight on your skin

trace its small disruptions through your hair
splendor of thigh under my hand
soft exhalation of breath on my cheek
the vast tumult of time spills open the hour

we fracture the radiant silence
at the still center of the moment
energy spreads like monarchs
let loose upon summer

in the reverberant language of stars
sultry nights and opal moons
filled with premonition
and the legacy of dreams

tenderly
slowly
I untangle the thought of you

A Perfect Liftoff

rain comes down
in translucent strings
pinging on the roof

in a dress the color
of a bruised eyelid
she dances in candlelight

her shadow flickers on the lawn
losing itself in damp leaves
her arms move through air

like wings unfurling
angled and awkward at first
then all grace and surprise

in one leap
she lifts away from
the clamor of rain

Plainsong

no houses barns or electric poles
string across the prairie no
bristle of tall buildings
pulling attention

in this frictionless landscape
spread vast and featureless
under a steepled sky
the eye drifts over rolling emptiness

the only movements
armada of full-sailed
flat-bottomed clouds speeding
bounty some otherwhere

and a susurrus breeze
in the ruffling buffalo grass
stirring seedpods on a golden wire
no fields or fence rows here

just breathing stillness
stranded in space

The Bridge

curve of stone over a river glinting
moments of brightness like stars
light on the water changes
the current has new shifts and breaks
spars and beams are strewn
like fractured bones
from an earlier noise that ruptured air
leaving so many lives undone

missiles whistle through the sky
scatter fire and ruin in the squares
in all quarters of the town
spirals of smoke, spokes of flame
wheel in tattered air

small live things vacate
roosts and burrows, eyes
round with the shine of fear
horses shriek their terror
teeth bared, eyes bulging
trees are shredded
children weep in the night

this bridge was broken in the last war
and not rebuilt

we wade to the park on purpose
with our dogs, picnic baskets,
babies and frisbees
we do not want to patch over and forget
the dark woebegone time of exploded hope
unmanageable grief
when we were bent double
splintered with pain and panic
felt the blind bulk of loss
the empty space where loved ones
once were
we want to learn from this
keep witness to the unimaginable
not have our children ever asking:
—this again?

**What a Strange Thing
is the Remedy of Beauty**

sun pours
full-throated morning
on birdwing clouds

blisters of light shine on leaves
still wet from last night's rain
an egret slides down a drift of wind

lands smoothly on the shallow pond
disturbing for a moment
its clear reflection of sky

walking a mile along
an old train trail bordered
by berries and lace-lichened oaks

my dog and I stop before
a Rainbow Eucalyptus tree
assembling and disassembling itself
like some great molting bird

there is an impressionist painting
of dappled blues, soft-daubed
pinks smooth as milk
under ribboned bark

damp shadows
where spiders knit webs
cocoons are spun

the Collie sniffs
the prodigious base
for news

I gaze upward
and outward
for mine

70 Miles on a Dirt Road

in the cold and wilted winter
flood of night, river of wind
I drive through the hole in the dark
my headlights make

sky breaks into stars
their brightness makes
darkness inexplicable

out of a lone tree
a wide-winged owl
white as the risen moon
hauls itself in sudden tilt
soundless through air

I move in a tunnel of vanishing visions
on the curve of the half seen
fox eyes flare red and purple ringed
stare an instant and quick disappear

barebacked horses in their pasture
leap into sight edge lit pale as skulls
empty rapid into memory

we are each here in the ageless dark
pursuing our quiet ends
moving through oceans of night
treading time

wide-eyed moon companionable
above and beside me
Orion steps lively across the horizon
the prairie unfolds in snapshots
bloom of dust rises behind me

when the tractor
at the corner of Flander's field
comes into sight I know
I am almost home

Intonations

there are voices beneath my voice
can you hear them
the little girl in the orchard
listening to light falling through trees

the mother's voice
high false broken over rocks
whispering I'm fine, I'm fine
the satin of her dress like petals
torn from their thorns

can you hear the coyote's howl
sound from the center
hurled through the throat
flies towards the bright bulb
of borrowed light

listen
these are echoes
in my song

remembered
like a scent
or an old secret

Some Days "The World is too Rich to be Eaten"
—*Patricia Highsmith, Her Diaries and Notebooks, 1941-1995*

lilies their tongues of light
float in curved bells
sound their white breath
in a sky of uncanny blue

sunlight sprawls over everything
claims objects to gild
rouse or illuminate
speaks in canticles of color

scent lays over the scene like vapor
carnations smell of cloves
peonies of sweet peppers
honeysuckle's an open window of summer

in this green hour
all the unraveled beauty
brushes my face
like a wet kiss

a pact has been made
with creation
all the colors
are cradled in truth

it's an arrow in the heart
to know how temporary I am
how short a time I have
to see all that is here
in the little garden of my life

I will only ask small questions today
the world is too big and bright for anything else

Margaret Rooney lives in Colorado, is a retired psychologist and former farmer and rancher. She belongs to two poetry groups of fabulous, accomplished women who encourage and inspire her. She says they help her grow as a person and a poet. She has been published in several *Redwood Writers Anthologies*, as well as *The Ekphrasis Journal, The California Quarterly, The Blue Unicorn, Reverberations I, II and III* and several other poetry journals and magazines. She won First Prize in The Redwood Writers Poetry Contest and two of her poems were nominated for a Pushcart Prize in 2022.